Made in the USA
Monee, IL
15 May 2022

96469290R00068